DATE DUE

3-12-03			311

Water

Andrew Charman

C.1 1998 *1498*

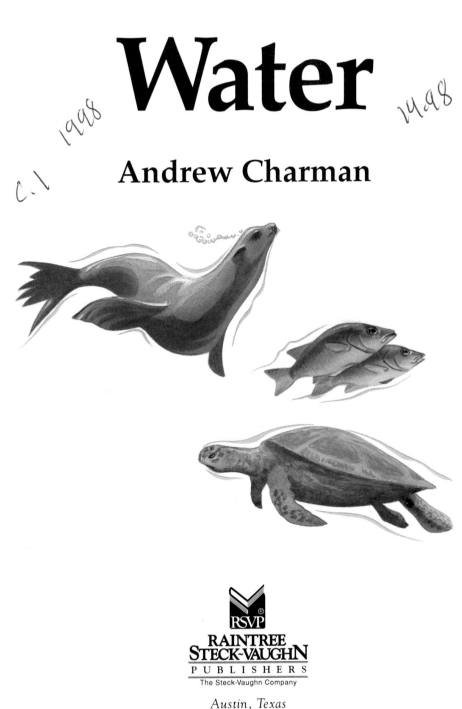

RSVP
RAINTREE
STECK-VAUGHN
P U B L I S H E R S
The Steck-Vaughn Company

Austin, Texas

Series Editor: Pippa Pollard
Editors: Claire Llewellyn and
    Kim Merlino
Design: Shaun Barlow
Project Manager and
Electronic Production:
    Julie Klaus
Artwork: Alec Hitchins
Cover artwork: Alec Hitchins
Picture Research:
    Ambreen Husain
Educational Advisor:
    Joy Richardson

Library of Congress
Cataloging-in-Publication Data
Charman, Andrew.
    Water / Andrew Charman.
      p.   cm. — (First starts)
    Includes index.
    Summary: Describes the Earth
    and its water, the forms of water,
    the water cycle, water for human
    and plant life. Includes a discussion
    of the water supply and protecting
    our water.
    ISBN 0-8114-5508-4
    1. Water — Juvenile literature.
[1. Water.]   I. Title.   II. Series.
GB662.3.C47 1994
553.7—dc20   93-20880
                                CIP
                                AC

Printed and bound in the
United States by Lake Book,
Melrose Park, IL

1 2 3 4 5 6 7 8 9 0 LB 98 97 96 95 94 93

Contents

The Watery Planet

From space you can see that very large areas of planet Earth are covered with water. Most of it is in the seas and oceans. This is salt water, which land animals cannot drink. Luckily, there is also a lot of fresh water. This is in lakes, rivers, ponds, and in the ground. Animals and plants need this water. They cannot live without it.

▽ The seas and oceans cover more of Earth's surface than the land.

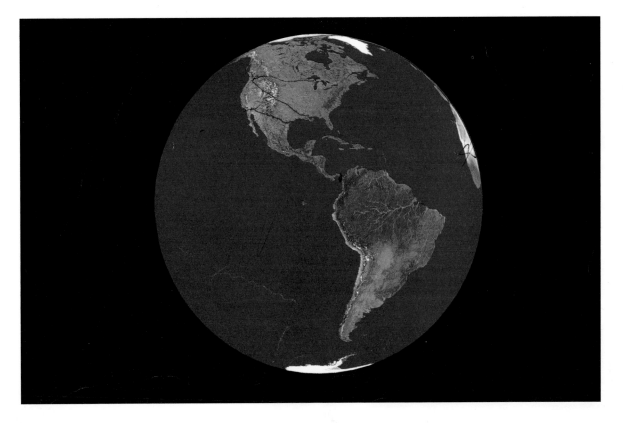

What Is Water?

Most things on Earth are solid, liquid, or a gas. Water is found on Earth in all three forms. When water gets very cold it becomes a solid called ice. Hot water becomes **water vapor**, which is a gas. Usually, water is a liquid. When water is liquid it is a very good **solvent**. Other substances mix with it easily.

▷ It is as a liquid that water is most useful to the plants and animals that live on Earth.

▷ Water vapor rises into the air and cools. It changes into droplets of water, which make clouds or low-lying fog.

▷ Mountaintops are very cold places. Some are covered with snow and ice.

The Water Cycle

There is always the same amount of water on Earth. It moves around the planet in a never-ending cycle. Water falls to the ground as rain. It then flows to the ocean along rivers and streams. The sun heats the ocean. Water rises into the air as a gas called water vapor. The vapor cools and makes bigger droplets. These fall to Earth as rain.

▷ Clouds contain droplets of water. A cloud "bursts" when the droplets become too heavy. They fall as rain.

▷ Rainwater drains off the land into rivers and streams. These flow to the ocean.

Water for Life

Our bodies are mostly water. Inside us, the **chemicals** that keep us alive are mixed with water. **Blood** moves these chemicals around our bodies. Blood, too, is mostly water.

Our bodies lose water when we breathe, sweat, and go to the toilet. This water must be replaced. We cannot live long without water.

▷ Water on our skin cools us. This is why we sweat when we are very active.

▷ The body of a jellyfish is almost completely made up of water.

▽ We need to
drink to replace the
water that is lost
from our bodies.

Plants and Water

Plants are able to make food for themselves in their leaves. To do this they need a gas called **carbon dioxide** from the air, and water from the soil. They also need sunlight. Plants soak up water through their roots. The food they make in the leaves travels around the plant in the sap. This sap, like an animal's blood, is mostly water.

▽ Some plants store water. This stops them from drying out.

◁ The roots of plants grow into the soil and soak up water. Roots are usually hidden underground. Here, the soil has been washed away and the roots can be seen.

▷ Mangrove trees grow in the tropics, where a river meets the ocean. Their many stiltlike roots support them in the soft, wet mud.

Life in the Ocean

Water flows to the ocean from the land. It contains many **mineral salts**. As the ocean is warmed by the sun, water vapor rises, but the salts remain. This makes the ocean salty.

The smallest living things in the ocean are called **plankton**. They float in the water and are food for many of the animals that live there.

▽ This is what plankton look like through a microscope.

▷ Fish, sharks, turtles, and sea lions have streamlined bodies which help them move through water.

▽ In spite of their huge size, many whales feed on tiny plankton.

▽ Squid move along by sucking up water and blowing it out quickly.

Life in Fresh Water

Rainwater does not contain the salts that are in the ocean. It is called fresh water and is good to drink. When rain falls on land it is soaked up by the soil and collects in lakes and ponds. Rainwater flows into streams and rivers. Few creatures can live in water that flows very quickly. Where the water slows down, plants can grow and animals live among them.

▽ Most salmon live in saltwater. Yet, they return to their home in freshwater rivers to lay eggs.

▷ Water flows downhill to the ocean. A waterfall is a sudden drop from a high place in a river or stream.

▽ The still waters of ponds are home to many different kinds of plants and animals.

Dragonfly

Newt

Frog

Pond skater

Water scorpion

Water lily

Water boatman

Great diving beetle

Pike

Great pond snail

Leech

15

Ice

Water freezes and turns into ice at a temperature of 32 degrees **Fahrenheit** (0° Centigrade). When the air is below freezing, snow falls instead of rain. In the coldest places snow and ice never melt. This happens on high mountain peaks and near the North and South Poles. Plants cannot grow there. Only a few animals can survive the bitter cold.

▷ Some lands near the poles are covered with thick ice. Where the ice reaches over the ocean, a chunk may break away. This floating ice is called an iceberg.

△ Polar bears live near the North Pole on drifting ice. Their white fur matches the ice and makes them hard to see.

▽ Penguins and seals are among the few animals that live near the South Pole. Both have a thick layer of fat under their skin to keep them warm.

△ Lichens are plantlike living things. They grow close to the North Pole, where it is too dry and too cold for plants.

17

Life with Little Water

Deserts are places where rain rarely falls. There is very little liquid water in the ground. The huge areas of ice at the **Poles** are cold deserts. Other kinds of deserts are baking hot. They are huge areas of dry rock and gravel or sand. The plants and animals that live in hot deserts can survive on small amounts of water for a long time.

▷ A camel can hold a lot of water in its stomach. These camels live in the Sahara desert in North Africa.

▷ Desert rains fall suddenly and then stop. Some plants store large amounts of water in their roots or stems. The Saguaro cactus can soak up and store huge amounts of water in its stem.

▽ The gerboa keeps
cool in its burrow
during the heat of
the desert day.

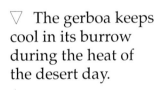

Water Changes Things

Moving water has a powerful force. Over many years it can break down large rocks into small pieces. Fast-flowing rivers carve deep valleys into the land. The sea crashes against the land and slowly wears it away. These actions are called **erosion**.

At the mouth of a river, the opposite happens. Mud in the water drops to the riverbed and piles up, making new land. This is called **silting**.

▷ Where the land is steep, rivers move downhill very fast. Fast-moving water can carry a lot of rocks and soil.

▽ As a river nears the ocean, it slows down and the rocks and soil settle to the bottom. The slow-moving water cannot carry as much soil and rocks as fast-moving water.

▽ The power of
waves slowly wears
away the softer
rocks along the
coast. This forms
remarkable shapes.

Floating and Sinking

Some things float in water, others sink. A type of thing (or substance) floats when it is less dense than water. This means that an amount of the substance is lighter than the same amount of water. Air is less dense than water. Things that are filled with air will float. Substances will sink if they are more dense than water. Most stone is denser than water and will sink.

▽ Even a ship as large as this one will float while it has plenty of air inside it. If it is overloaded, however, it will sink.

▽ Ice is less dense than water, but not by very much. An iceberg will float, but most of it is under water.

◁ Submarines contain tanks that are filled with air. The submarine sinks when the tanks are filled with water.

Water Supply

People need water to drink and to grow **crops** for food. In some countries, people have to walk a long way to collect water from a well. Wells reach water under the ground. Then the people have to carry the water back to their homes and fields. In other countries, rainwater is stored in **reservoirs**. It is cleaned and then piped to people's homes.

▷ This woman lives in a small village where water is collected from a well with a rope and bucket. It may take many hours to get enough water for her family's needs.

▽ A reservoir looks like a lake, but it is man-made. A wall is built across a stream to hold the water back or store it.

▽ In dry areas, water from wells is pumped through pipes and canals to the fields. This is called irrigation.

Using Water

We use water in many ways. People have moved themselves and cargo in boats on water for over two thousand years. Moving water in rivers and streams has **energy**. It can be used to turn wheels to grind grain or make electrical power. Water can also be used to cool machinery. In many cars, water cools the engine.

▷ People use water to have fun. Water sports, like surfing, use the power of moving water for a fast ride.

◁ Water from a stream flows over this wheel, pushing it down so that it turns. The wheel is connected to stones that grind up wheat to make flour.

▽ We use water to wash and to keep us and our clothes clean. Water is a good solvent.

Keeping Water Clean

All living things need clean water, yet water can easily become **polluted**. This happens when harmful substances are mixed with it. The **chemicals** that are used in factories and by farmers can pollute our water. So can the **sewage** from toilets. Plants and animals cannot live in very polluted water. We need to protect clean water and not waste it.

▷ Water from factories, farms, and homes can be cleaned before it flows into the water supply. This clean water will not harm the plants and animals that live in this swamp.

▷ Harmful substances dumped in water travel far downstream and may make fish there dangerous for us to eat.

▽ Accidents on the ocean may cause oil spills. Oil is very harmful to wildlife.

Things to Do

- Make a study of the different kinds of water in your area. Are there ponds, lakes, and rivers? Look at the same area on a map. Can you see where rivers come together? How far away is the ocean?

- Experiment with boats made out of different materials. Can you make a boat that floats out of a lump of modeling clay? What happens to a floating egg carton if you fill one side with stones? What does this tell you about how boats are loaded?

- How many different uses of water can you discover? You might like to find pictures of as many uses as you can and make a display.

Glossary

Blood   The fluid that supplies the cells of our bodies with food and oxygen.

Carbon dioxide   A gas in air that plants use to make food. Animals breath it out.

Centigrade   A scale to measure how hot or cold something is. Water freezes at 0° C and boils at 100° C.

Chemicals   Everything is made of chemicals. Some chemicals are harmful to plants and animals.

Crops   The plants people grow for food, such as wheat and potatoes.

Energy   The ability to do work. Moving water has energy.

Erosion   The gradual wearing away of the land by water, wind, rain, or ice.

Fahrenheit   A scale to measure how hot or cold something is. Water freezes at 32° F and boils at 212° F.

Irrigation   Taking water from one place to another for growing crops.

Mineral salts   Some of the tiny pieces of rock and other substances that are washed off the land into the sea.

Plankton   Tiny plant-like and animal-like living things which float in the sea.

Poles   The frozen areas of land at the far North (the North Pole) and the far South (the South Pole) of the Earth.

Polluted   Spoiled by harmful substances.

Reservoir   A man-made lake where a large amount of water is stored.

Sewage   Human waste from toilets.

Silting   When tiny particles of rock and soil collect at the bottom of a river.

Solvent   A substance which will dissolve other substances easily.

Temperature   How hot or cold something is.

Water vapor   When water mixes with air it makes a gas called water vapor.

Index

Photographic credits: A.N.T./NHPA 17, 27; Bruce Coleman Limited 14; Ecoscene 29; Chris Fairclough Colour Library 9; Robert Harding Picture Library 5; Hutchison Library 25; Trevor McDonald/NHPA 10; Okapia/Oxford Scientific Films 21; Tom Van Sant/Geosphere Project, Santa Monica/Science Photo Library 3; Zefa Picture Library 7, 13, 19, 22.